Funny Signs

Hilarious messages from Africa and beyond

Photographed by the readers of *Getaway*

RS&P

Published by Ramsay Son and Parker
Cape Town, South Africa

First published in 1999 by
Ramsay Son and Parker (Pty) Ltd
Uitvlugt, Howard Drive,
Pinelands 7405, South Africa

ISBN 0 620 24643 X

Compiled by David Steele
Edited by David Bristow
Designed by Jane Eagar

Reproduced, printed and bound by Creda Communications (Pty) Ltd,
Epping II, Cape Town

Introduction

Getaway magazine, which recently celebrated its 10th anniversary, has been described by advertising guru Bob Rightford as the "South African publishing phenomenon of the century." Foremost of the many things other local publishers may envy about the magazine is its remarkable relationship with its readers.

In every issue, readers share with each other their experiences and love of Africa. Interesting new letters and photographs arrive on the editor's desk every day and through these useful advice is passed on and humourous experiences are shared. Typically, it was readers who started the 'funny signs' phenomenon rather than *Getaway* photojournalists.

This book, therefore is a result of—and a tribute to—their efforts.

But it is also a recognition of the spirit of enterprise among the mostly rural African people. While some of the signs might amuse us in their naivety or ignorance of English grammar, let no one say we are mocking those who made them. On the contrary, we salute their ingenuity, skills and spirit. Much the same could be said for people in other continents. We admire the way they try to communicate with us (often all-too-arrogant) English-speaking people when English is not their home language.

We're sure the relationship between *Getaway* and its readers will continue to thrive and hope that photos of funny signs will keep on flooding the editor's desk, so that we may soon be able to produce a second edition.

We also hope you enjoy reading the book as much as we enjoyed compiling it.

David Steele

This book was made possible by—and is dedicated to—the loyal readers of *Getaway*.

Contents

The great African shopping experience

Mark Boekstein (Tamboerskloof) was a *Getaway* monthly prize winner with his signs—including this jewel. Do some shops sell 'uncleen' toilet paper? Read on. . . .

S*ies*! You can't be serious! Burgher Barnard (Pretoria) came across this advert outside a supermarket in New Germany, near Durban.

This scene has become a perennial favourite among our readers. Nikki Walker (Lanseria) was hesitant to buy the mini-market's take aways wondering if, after eating them, a coffin would also be necessary.

Although the original sign had been tampered with, contriving the humour somewhat, it gave Martin Trimmer (Milnerton)—and other readers who've sent us the same photo—a good laugh.

The numerous worm sellers (and their signs) on the road between Harare and Kariba are a popular subject for our intrepid photographers and James Varden (Harare) also admired this pair's marketing strategy.

It seems that in these hard times even thieves are experiencing difficulties . . . Anton Geyser (Potchefstroom), always on the lookout for funny signs, was surprised to find one in his home town.

Dedza Pottery can be found at the village of Dedza in Malawi. Frank and Lorna Rautenbach (Barberton) were not only amused by this sign, but very impressed with the customer service.

The great African shopping experience

Until he saw this sign outside a shop in Fort Beaufort, Andrew Potgieter (Uitenhage) always thought he understood the meaning of 'cash and carry'. . . .

Braai wood and charcoal fresh from the farm? Whatever next? Actually, like L Wessels (Grabouw), we find wood that's had a little time to dry a lot easier to light.

Unfortunately, PT van der Walt (Pretoria) never told us exactly where he found this sign or even whether the 'sheap' were 'cheep'.

The people of Klerksdorp must surely love their old roses, believes Tony Archer (Flamwood), who came across this while cycling through the town.

What made Nancy Robson (Oshikango, Namibia) smile is that poor financial administration has already ensured the end of this 'everlasting' project!

It's really fresh and saves on transport as well, as the residents of West Nicolson in Zimbabwe have found out. Captured for us by Dr HA Grové (Germiston).

She wasn't cold enough to be eligible for parking, so Ms LD Hickman of East London moved on to avoid prosecution.

We've received several photos of Pick 'n Pay supermarkets in the bundu, but this Mozambique example, taken by Lee and Kerstin Whittam (Nelspruit), was our favourite.

During a trip to the Hazyview area, Adv Réan Strydom wondered if, once established, this shop-to-be would be a threat to the other shops advertised behind.

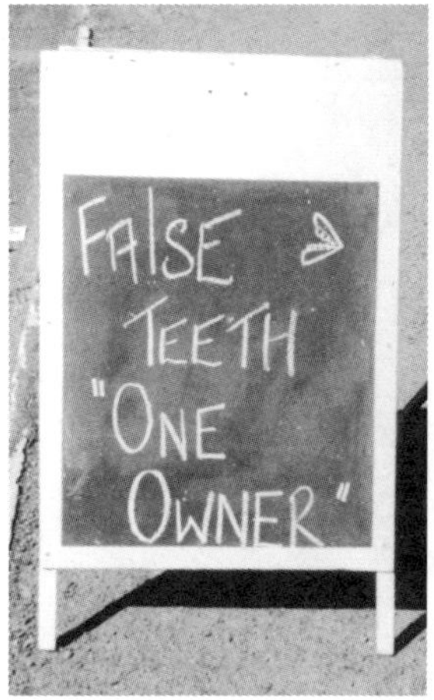

John Suter (Benoni)—and a few other readers—came across this sign in Eshowe in KwaZulu-Natal.

At least they are honest . . . thought André Henning (Windhoek) as he photographed this sign at Vioolsdrif near the South African–Namibian border.

Where would you find another bar with a view like this? Chris Adams (Pietermaritzburg) thought the price well worth the stop just south of Port St Johns in the Eastern Cape.

The great African shopping experience

Every half-price sale should carry a warning, says Kate Miller (Greenpoint), who found this one outside Exclusive Books at Cape Town's Waterfront.

Mr JA Joubert (Groblersdal) feels that this optometrist in his town—with a 24-hours spares department—must be a very popular place for people with eye problems, and they can have a Coke too. . . .

Oh well, at least it saves you asking. Mrs M Winkel (Amanzimtoti) found this sign at a nursery near Masvingo in Zimbabwe.

Have you tasted any good snoek juice lately? If not, you might like to try this shop in Worcester, where Alan Meiring (Garsfontein) found a supply.

Talk about carrying coals to Newcastle! Gail and Martyn Garrett (Midrand) found this sign in Standerton, while battling to get to Durban through the snow.

After a number of months of travel, this was a welcome sign for G Schaefer (Muizenberg). He found it in Chipata, on the Zambian-Malawi border.

The great African shopping experience

Shopping in Africa sometimes has its advantages—as John Maconachie (Claremont) has discovered.

They also have fresh eggs at a garage in Cato Ridge—not to mention some explicit advertising—according to Brian Smith (Durban).

Nick Jonas (Potchefstroom) is not sure whether *moerse* constitutes bad language; we think it's beautifully descriptive for our favourite snack.

Errol Scarr (Westville) often wondered why this shop in Charlesville, on the Mpumalanga-KwaZulu-Natal border, had such a strange name. Then he found out.

"Who could resist filling up with fresh farm petrol?" asks Mike Bentley (Linton Grange). Once a hoot, now this type of sign is fairly common.

While travelling through Namibia and Botswana, Safiyya Kadwa (Azaadville) ran into trouble at Bagani. We know the feeling!

Christine de Villiers (Ingogo) found this severely dyslexic sign 20 kilometres outside Ulundi in KwaZulu-Natal.

It's difficult to translate the wording on this sign, at a garage just outside the entrance to Sun City, so we thought it safer not to try! From Dr Deon Ferreira (Hennopsmeer).

Services that just might come in handy

Mervyn and Leona Clarke (East London) were not sure exactly what this centre in Nairobi did, but wondered if it had anything to do with the adjacent ear-piercing stall.

Pieter and Joan de Wet (Machadodorp) believe the proprietors of this local enterprise understand the fundamentals of good business: create the market then satisfy the need.

It's unusual to find a free service, let alone one that's open 24 hours a day. But then, when you have to go. . . .

Regular travellers in Africa get used to this kind of thing. JW Prince (Lydenburg) found this one near his home town in Mpumalanga.

Joan van Rooyen (Nylstroom) came across this multi-talented doctor's sign in Underberg in KwaZulu-Natal; she didn't tell us whether she took advantage of any of the services!

If you've got any 'problemas' or 'illnes', Gavin Baines (Bryanston) knows exactly where you should go: Rundu in the Caprivi.

Taking things too far: this sign, photographed by Neville Higgs (Weltevreden Park) in Ghana, would be funny if it wasn't so sad.

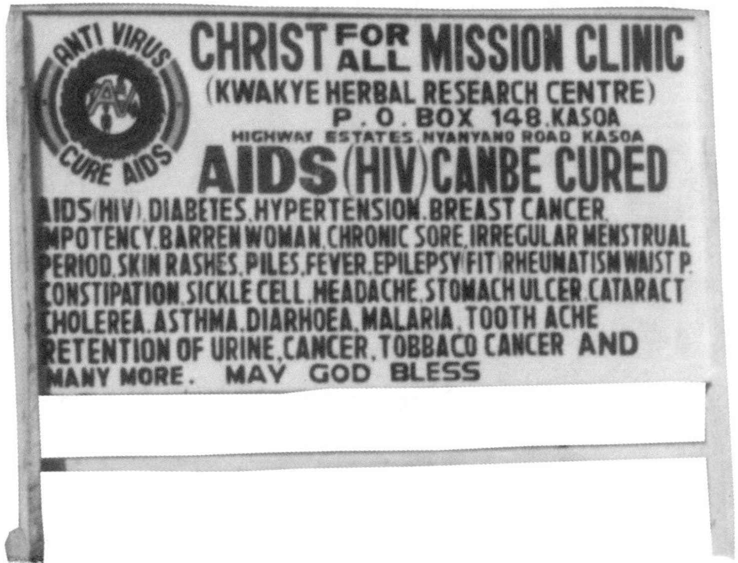

Services that just might come in handy

Shelley Nash (Parow North) was astonished to find out what you could buy at this escort agency—in Bloemfontein of all places!

And you thought people went to game lodges just to see the Big Five? So did Bernie Munks (Umdloti Beach) until he saw this sign.

A place to build up steam? Mr G Ehlers (Dundee) found this intriguing station outside Katima Mulilo in Namibia's Eastern Caprivi.

After finding this sign, Mrs DK Lee was left wondering just what goes on in Paarl.

After a passing prankster added his bit of graffiti to Ronnie se Shop near Barrydale it had become quite a landmark when Mrs A Finlayson (Montagu) snapped it. So much so that the once-simple store is now a popular weekend restaurant.

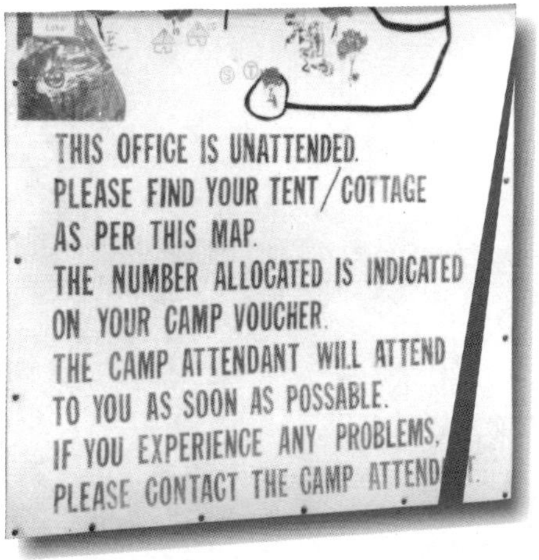

Gail and Martyn Garrett never realised camping in South Africa was so confusing until they saw this sign in Pilanesberg National Park.

While on safari through Damaraland and the Kaokoveld, Bettina von Mallinckrodt (Swakopmund) came across this 'office' in the wasteland. Office for what? It was closed so they never found out.

The reception at Poppa Falls in Namibia tickled the fancy of Margaux Johnstone (Rustenburg) while . . .

. . . the new office, with its superb air conditioning, really impressed her!

Services that just might come in handy

After seeing this sign in the Kruger Park, Nici Koekemoer (Witbank) felt the 'product' should perhaps be sold in the Far East as a substitute for rhino horn.

Had it not been for the electric clippers hanging in the 'window', Barto S du Plessis (Pretoria) would never have realised this is a barber's shop.

Is this an aspirant Plettenberg Bay photographic entre-preneur planning ahead for expansion? John Houghton (Kleinzee) discovered this little gem.

Piet Kruger (Hekpoort) found this near Vredenburg, 20 kilometres from the sea. Two weeks later they still hadn't found a customer.

R650 seems a bit expensive for a pair of overalls—even for clutching. From André van Rensburg (Umhlali).

You'll find this useful service in Katutura, Windhoek, Namibia. From D Schusdziara (Wilhelmshaven, Germany).

It seems money can buy anything in Africa. From Colin and Barbara Meadows (Shashe, Botswana).

Is this a retreat on the Cape Flats for professional boxers? From Willem Hoek (Marina da Gama).

Next time you pass through Fouriesburg in the Free State, consider a car wash. It looks good, smells good. . .

. . . and the proprietor is obviously open to negotiation on the price. From Jacques Mostert (Fouriesburg).

Travelling in Africa

Telling it like it is—but note that 'attention is prohibited'. This warning was seen at Maputo Airport by Jacques and Therine van Niekerk (Somerset West).

Steve Mackie (Randburg) tells us this photo was taken at Maun Airport, Botswana, where "travellers are filtered through to the Okavango".

The thought of an airline office in a train amused André du Preez (Hazyview) so much he just had to share this photo with us.

Mrs B Wright (Port Elizabeth) is still concerned about what sort of people land at Durban Airport while . . .

. . . **A**liåå Moore (Kirstenhof) is still wondering exactly where the air-craft are meant to land at Trennery's hotel in the old Transkei.

'**D**omestic Departures' at Delta Camp in the Okavango, Botswana, sent in by Carol-Ann Lambert (Stellenbosch).

Travelling in Africa

Not only did Trevor Foster (East London) enjoy seeing Livingstone's Statue at Victoria Falls, but also the one of a 'living stone'.

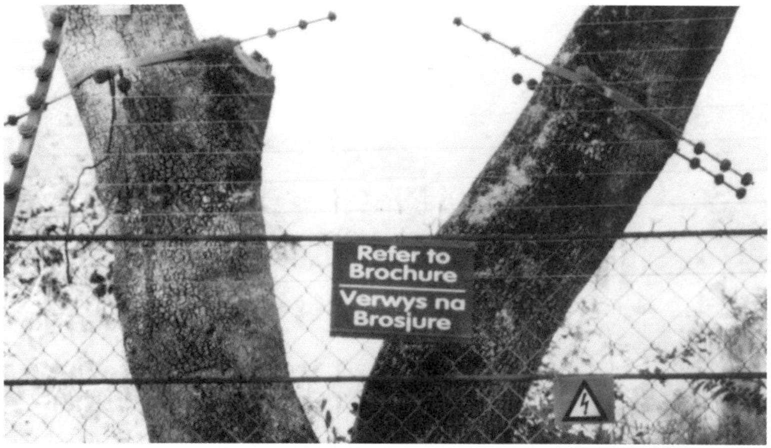

Carrol and Jo Blignaut (Perth, Australia) didn't have a clue what this informative sign in the Kruger Park was all about, or which brochure they should refer to. And nor do we.

René Risch was pleasantly surprised, after seeing this 'warning' in Swaziland, to find Jeppe's Reef border post one of the most efficient she'd ever come across.

While spending a weekend in Humansdorp, Pieter and Santje van Kradenburg (Nelspruit) found things a little topsy-turvy.

This puzzling sign was taken by Brian Roman (Landsdowne) at the Carousel entertainment centre near Pretoria. It's certainly a time-honoured way of settling gambling disputes.

In Western Zambia the flies are so big they have landing strips, while Niël van Schalkwyk (Warden) is still trying to work out what a 'capesite' is. . . .

Travelling in Africa

After a disappointing trip in Botswana, Jafta Englelbrecht (Vereeniging) felt this is the operator she should have used.

Mrs S Cruz (Parkhurst) found this sign in Blantyre, Malawi. You soon discover that warm-hearted Malawians would rather confuse you with contradictions than not try to assist a visitor.

In Mauritius nothing—not even trespassing—is a problem when there's a friendly islander around. Photographed by Trish Rudolf (Zevenwacht) near Belle Mare Plage.

Sally Mackenzie, who came across this sign in the Drakensberg, wondered if she'd stumbled on a new form of outdoor activity in South Africa.

Rob Mullett (Kenridge) wonders whether his friend Lily Forbes broke any of the rules by taking this photo in Namibia's Fish River Canyon.

Hiking above Witsieshoek Mountain Resort in the Drakensberg, DH Pieterse (Edenglen) contemplated these novel grammatical interpretations of his favourite Greek philosopher.

Leone Kruger (Warmbad) is ashamed to admit that her group were all 'lazy and fat' the first time they tackled the Vlakvark Hiking Trail near Orighstad in Mpumalanga.

What housemaster Elwyn van den Aardweg (Pretoria Boys High School) found particularly appropriate about this photo he took in Lesotho was that the students in the group were facing their matric exams.

Eating and drinking in Africa

The New Look Restaurant, photographed by LD Harrison (Newcastle) in Livingstone, Zambia, certainly has a different look about it. . . .

Jan Coetzee and Kim Walker (Gordons Bay) found the food good at Restaurant in Paradise at Nakhata Bay in Malawi—but never said whether they 'grew more'.

The joke about 'Tummy Filling Check Point' on the road from Nairobi to Nanyuki in Kenya was that there was absolutely nothing with which to fill your tummy. From Diana von Holdt (Somerset East).

We've been reassured by BJ Hartzenberg (Duiwelskloof) that there's no need to take sandwiches on the way to Walvis Bay in Namibia.

Mrs AM Waterhouse (Big Bend, Swaziland) has found a prison office with a sense of humour in her home town.

Even though Vincent Wiegers (Harderwÿk, Netherlands) found his way into this Pretoria branch of Nandos blocked, he had to admit they were friendly about things.

With a breakfast this long, even the most hungry traveller will be satisfied. Colleen McDiarmid didn't mention whether she sampled the feast.

Eating and drinking in Africa

Paul and Jane Thompson (Gwynedd, Wales) were somewhat surprised—and amused—by this sign at Skukuza in the Kruger National Park.

Not only is the service good at Kongolana Hotel in Northern KwaZulu-Natal, but so is the after-sales service. From Allen Muller (Vryheid).

Whether this clinic near the golf club in Lilongwe, Malawi (where much drinking is done), actually has a cure is debatable according to IV MacAndrew (Hilton). Hair of the dog?

When Don and Joan Reynolds saw this sign at Todd's Motel in Zimbabwe, they decided not to risk the special because they didn't fancy suffering until the Thursday.

This Afrikaans message captured by Gwynneth Glass (Thornton) is a portion of a strange café-trading store mural in Mapoetsoe, Lesotho. The mural also incorporates Table Mountain and the sea!

The name of this fast-food outlet in Pretoria may be inappropriate, but Peter Apps (Onderstepoort) assures us the food is delicious.

Gary Collard (Scottsville) found these local children selecting their soft drinks near Moremi in Botswana.

In Beaufort West you may be able to breakfast on bones, ice and fat, but Roelof van Weele (Pretoria) prefers the usual bacon and eggs.

African English

"If you 'wish' to have 'bugs' in your take 'a' ways, this café is the place to go," advises Walter Pretorius (Lynwood) .

Marina Coetzee (Windhoek) sent us this photo taken by her Dad. The springs, waterfall and crystal-clear pool at Ongongo are a welcome change from the dusty tracks in Damaraland and Marina absolutely agrees that it's a 'nise nity rest camp'.

For readers wishing to see a 'nuw pedrified forets', why not try Twyfelfontein in Namibia, just like Grant Walker-Campbell (Daleside, Randvaal)?

These signs, captured by Steve Cunliffe (Llandudno) at a Zambian passport-control office, promote the need for more government revenue. After reading other signs on this spread, we can't guarantee the mistakes are intentional.

Anton and Tessie van Zydam (Piet Retief) discovered this corner café in Quelimane, Mozambique, but didn't say whether the 'take haways' were as 'hamusing' as the sign.

While enjoying a stroll through Cairo recently, Dan de Vries (Kroonstad) was very 'habby' to come across this friendly sign.

We hope all 'toerists' will take heed of this friendly bilingual request. Thea Harding (Pongola) did and thanks all Namaqualanders for sharing their paradise.

AF Cogan (Harare) confessed to being a little confused by this sign at the airport at Tabora in Tanzania—where David Livingstone once lived.

African English

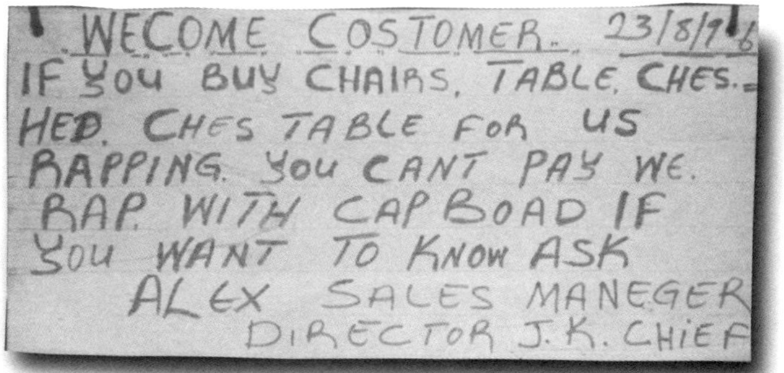

Deuel Raubenheimer's (Krugersdorp) rough translation of this reads: "Welcome customer! If you buy one of our chairs, tables or chessboards, we shall wrap it for you with cardboard free of charge. For any further details ask Alex (Sales Manager/Director/Chief)."

In case you battle to read this, Geoff Muller (Randburg) has worked it out: "Please, this is your butchery. Here is sold bloody good meat."

A lot of information in a few words at a camp site in the Ugab river bed, Namibia, which Willem de Wet (Henties Bay) has translated: "(Open since) 1996. *Jy kan mooi slaap. As jy hier slaap betaal N$15.* You pay me N$15—when you sleep here I want this slip. Namibian dollars and South African Rand accepted. Hi, you are now at Ugab camp!"

Annette Weber (Oranjezicht) was disappointed that by the time she had figured out this sign at Uroa Bay in Zanzibar, her holiday was over. . . .

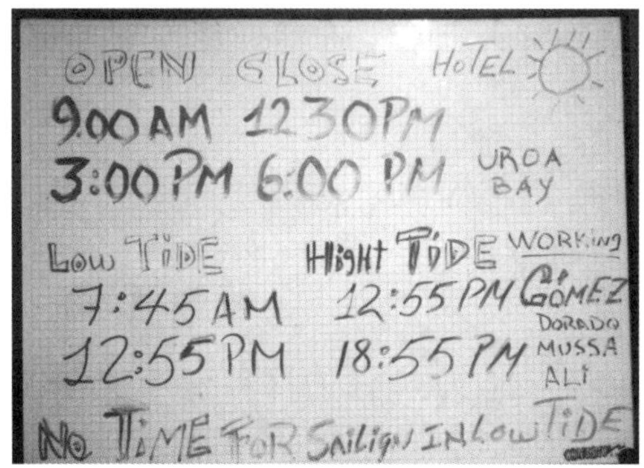

After seeing this sign on one of their African holidays, Nicoleen and Frik van Rensburg (Ellisras) wondered whether topless ladies could cause a heart attack or two.

Superhumans? James and Debbie Miller were almost arrested while attempting to photograph this sign outside a bank at the town of Victoria Falls.

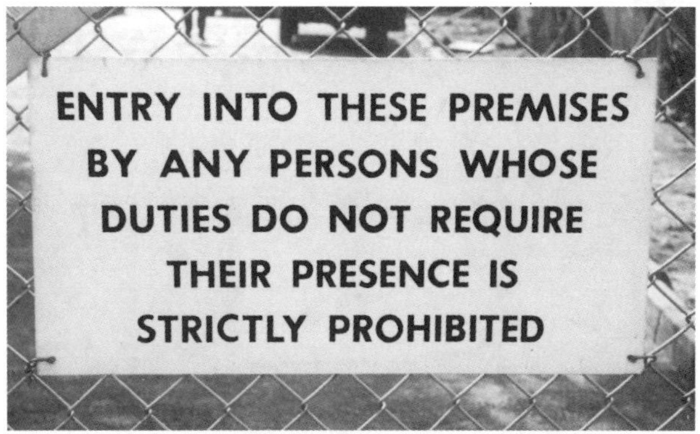

Dr Sandy Shaw (Addis Ababa, Ethiopia) was amused by this sign at Gurgusum Beach in Eritrea. But how many times haven't you been annoyed by fellow holidaymakers 'reserving' prime spots round the pool and then not using them?

Even though 'halfnakedness' and 'constumes' are strongly discouraged at the YMCA pool at Moshi in the foothills of Kilimanjaro, Brigid Schulz (Sandringham, Johannesburg) still enjoyed her Sunday mornings there while on a short contract in Tanzania.

You have been warned . . .

This strategically placed cannon and sign near Nieu-Bethesda was one that got us thinking about the 'Getaway sign of the month' competition and also made Leon Quenet (Rondebosch) a monthly winner.

A clear sign with a clear warning. But how on earth can poachers be shot if shooting is prohibited? Photographed near Naboomspruit in the Waterberg by BA Goetsch (Potgietersrus).

Ivor Bester (Observatory) finds this sign at Zeekoevlei a hilarious piece of ambiguity in our rainbow nation.

Jan and Leonie Stone (Strand), among other readers, found this 'grave' warning while walking in the Featherbed Nature Reserve near Knysna.

While Henties Bay might be a quiet little Namibian coastal town, G Ehlers (Dundee) was left with absolutely no doubt about what would happen to 'trespasers'— or 'survivers'.

Janet Burns (Philadelphia) confirmed that Broadlands Farm near Sir Lowry's Pass does indeed have chimps, friendly dogs and agapanthus.

Considering the shark attacks along the Eastern Cape coast, the subtle alteration made by a local to this sign in East London, photographed by another East Londoner, Jannie Lochrenberg, may be appropriate.

You have been warned . . .

A sign at Orapa, Botswana, that is sure to keep trespassers away. Taken by Jurgens Weidemann (Potchefstroom) on his way to Moremi.

Marlene Nel (Stellenbosch), along with many other readers who've sent in the same photo, certainly took note of this dire warning to keep Henties Bay clean.

Four of *Getaway*'s younger readers were so amused by this sign at Nata Lodge that they took the photo especially for us. From Mark and Jane Wilson, and Nicholas and Dubie Malan.

What is worse, being polluted at Orapa or 'vervolg' near Donkerhoek, close to Pretoria? Whatever, neither André nor Elize Zybrands (Pretoria) wished to find out.

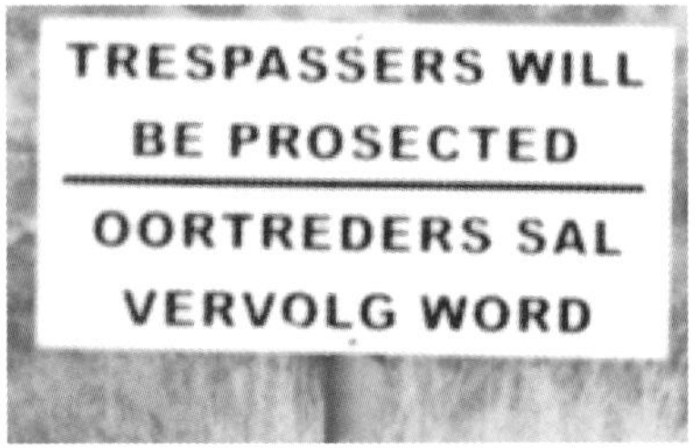

It's understandable that tres-passers irritate Namaqualand farmers, but is it the 'stealers' or the 'strollers' who're going to get shot, asks Elsa Smith (Faerie Glen).

The wording says: "Warning no bungie jumping from this bridge". L de Wet (Boksburg) was one of several readers who took the time to photograph it.

Confronted by this double hazard, Jan Greeff (Barberton) wondered whether it would be worse to drown or be ordered to contract bilharzia by the secretary of water affairs.

As James Goble (Westville) found out, nothing is a problem in Mauritius and there's also no beating about the bush with an important message like this.

This amusing sign on a byway in the Karoo is another favourite among our readers, but it was Ilse van Hemert's (Oaklands) photo we chose.

You have been warned . . .

While on a 4x4 safari in the Soutpansberg, Louis Potgieter (Koppies) made absolutely sure he closed this bloody gate!

While driving in the Namib-Naukluft Park in Namibia, Michelle Oosthuizen (Montana-park) wasn't sure which sign to believe.

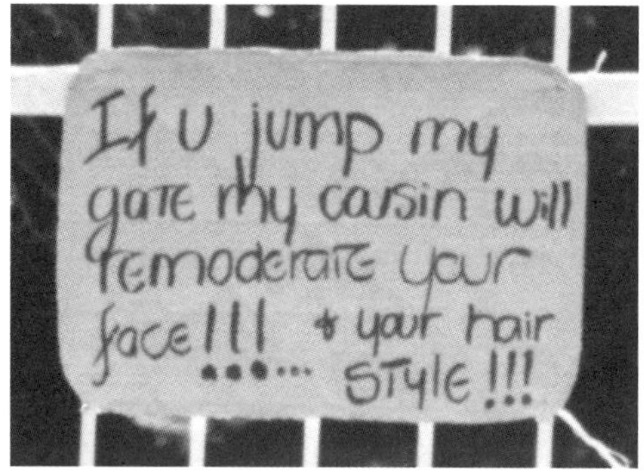

Chris Barnes (Benoni) didn't jump this gate in Katima Mulilo and is still wondering exactly what a remoderated face and hairstyle would do for him.

Unfortunately Frikkie was not at home when Diana Husselmann (Somerset West) called—otherwise she'd have taken him up on his offer.

When you run a courier service in Rustenburg, the last thing you need is someone blocking your ...@#%*{}@ gate. From H Cronje (Rustenburg).

Elaine Taylor (Windhoek) believes the state of repair of this gate in Damaraland, Namibia, may cause the draughty conditions which necessitate keeping all doors closed.

Please keep off the grass

Numerous readers, including Jennifer Naude (Rosettenville), have sent in a photo of this classic sign at Vioolsdrif near the South African-Namibian border.

Try as he may, Tom Bentley (Kempton Park) couldn't find the grass at the Kokstad Town Gardens in KwaZulu-Natal.

'Berging' obviously did the trick, advise Sue and John Lederle (Constantia), who found the lawn at this hotel in Kasane, Botswana, in good shape.

What a way to treat women

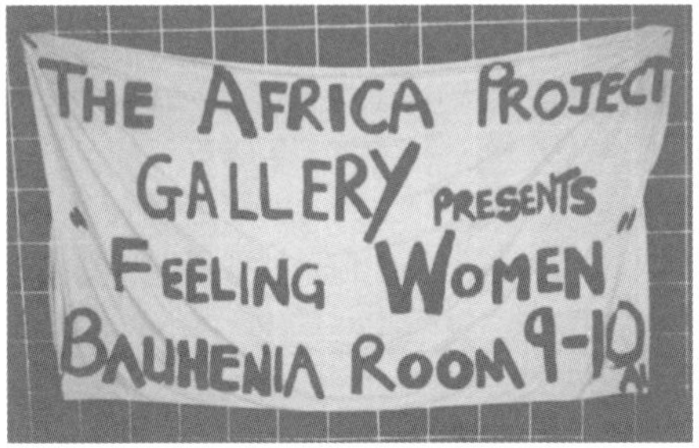

"Looks like a fun meeting!" commented Dwight Allen (Harare), who took this photo at his local Sheraton Hotel.

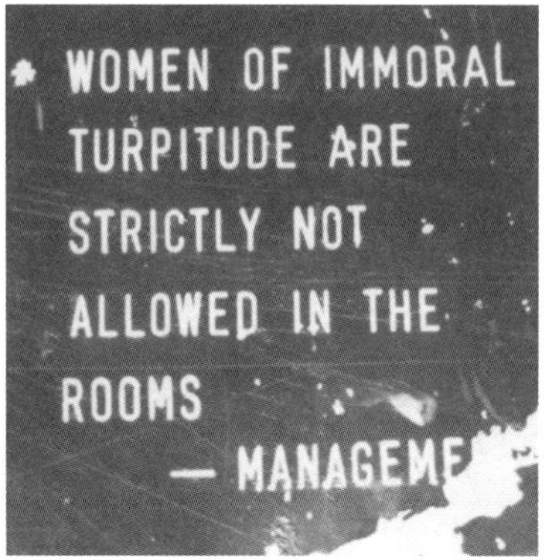

Nikki and Anthony Dunne (Durban), who saw this at the Safari Inn at Dar-es-Salaam in Tanzania, explain the meaning of turpitude as 'extreme depravity' or 'wickedness'.

When Jill Bell (Kempton Park) visited Vanguard Mine in Zimbabwe, where she used to live, she found this sign on the gate of the guesthouse.

We thought this might be worth a try . . . but AJ Burger (Pretoria) never told us exactly where we could find the shop.

José Janssen (Phalaborwa) discovered this sign on one of the houses in Humulani, a camp for Mozambican refugees, in his town.

On entering this shop in Bergville in KwaZulu-Natal Nancy Robson (Ohangwena, Namibia) found hardly any goods inside—including the wife.

Although North Queensland in Australia is mango country, Barbara Calderwood (Kloof) couldn't work this out.

Nice place, Saudi Arabia: a sign taken there by Mrs MC Geldenhuys (Pretoria).

This school-type prank photographed at Tshokwane in the Kruger National Park by Juanita Jamneck (Pretoria), is another great favourite among *Getaway* readers.

Bank manager Don Bradfield (Margate) has to be particularly careful when he calls on his clients along the Natal South Coast!

Children

Think about this message photographed by Garth Livingstone (Benmore) at Muusha Primary School outside Chimanimani in Zimbabwe's Eastern Highlands. . . .

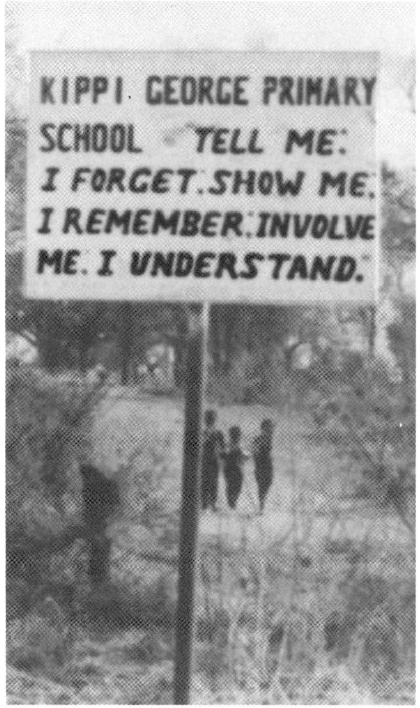

How true: on her way to Zambia, Jenny Lodge (Monte Vista) reflected on this sign in the Caprivi Strip.

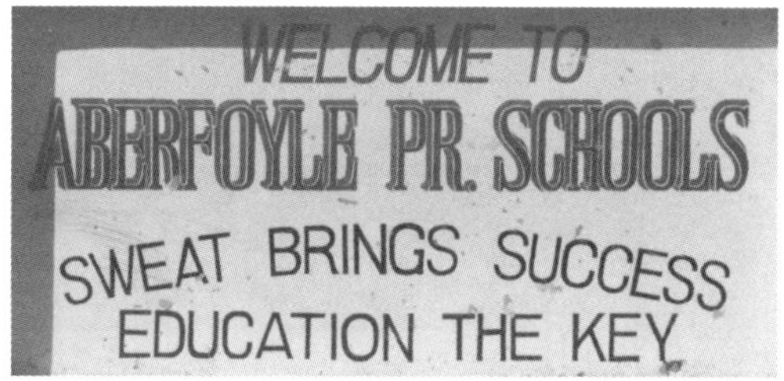

Ms L Mortimer (Harare) came across this hard-working mine primary school in the Eastern Districts of Zimbabwe.

Grahame McLeod (Tonota, Botswana) discovered this dire warning outside the bar at Gweta Rest Camp in Northern Botswana.

While driving down a farm road in the KwaZulu-Natal Midlands, DB Machray came across this symbol of free-ranging country humour.

Keeping in touch

Debbie Bosman (Grabouw) had a chuckle at the way the post office in Rumphi, Malawi, sorts its mail.

Timo Rebel (Centurion) discovered the take-away phone booth concept in use at Livingstone International Airport in Zambia.

Have you ever seen a post box out of order? Roy Clark (Centurion) has . . . at Ais Ais in Nambia.

Having seen this sign for several months, Mr CJ van der Walt (Port Elizabeth) wondered whether the GPO was waiting for carpets or curtains. . . .

Lavatory humour

On a recent trip to Cape Town, Jacqueline Wege (Kloof) came across these two conveniences outside St George's Cathederal. The seating is understood to be comfortable but the view somewhat lacking. . . .

OG Malan (Stellenbosch) says his photograph proves indisputably that the 'toi-toi' is not a traditional African dance as generally assumed, but developed in the Czech Republic in response to a pressing need.

With baked beans a staple diet of some overlanders, William Baker (Ipswich, England) must have wondered exactly what wind these signs at the privy at Loitokitok Springs in Ngorongoro Crater referred to.

This sign at a caravan park in the Drakensberg is probably not what you want to see if you're desperate, but Rose van Olst (Benoni) explained that it referred to a restaurant next door.

Many *Getaway* readers, including Einar Røssaak (Åledund, Norway) have sent us photos of this sign. In Einar's case, his group had just seen seven cheetahs and followed instructions to stay in their car.

While walking through the Mining Town at the Kimberley's Big Hole, Hannelie van der Merwe (Durbanville) said she studied the main sign for some time before she realised what it actually meant.

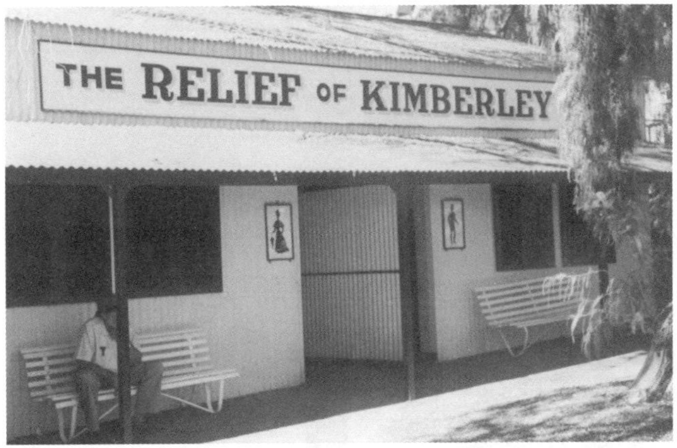

Lavatory humour

Oh dear! During a recent trip to Mozambique Chris Ras (Tzaneen) came across this explicit sign at the Komatipoort border post.

You don't have to travel to exotic places to find amusing signs says Connie Schulz, who took this picture on the outskirts of Senekal in the Free State.

Travelling from Cape Town to Nelspruit requires more stops than just for fuel, points out Stephan Pieterse (Somerset West).

Bergh Robbins (Gaborone, Botswana) felt readers might find this sign in Zimbabwe's Matobos scatty. . . .

Ten kilometres to Onseepkans in Namibia was a kilometre too far for this little chap photographed by De Villiers Greeff (Germiston).

There seems to be no end to the efficiency in the United States, as Bob MacDonald (Somerset West) discovered while visiting Logan Airport at Boston.

Marge Bamford (Farramere) hopes her photo tickles your sense of humour as much as the subject (at a coffee shop in Killarney, Ireland) tickled hers.

Is Totnes in Devon (where this sign was spotted on the Great Western Railway platform) the cross-dressing capital of England? wondered Tony Fisher (Hillcrest Park).

Kim Pearce (Durban) was somewhat surprised by this sign at the end of a narrow little street in Venice.

There's no beating about the bush in China. Grant Lemke (Sunninghill) found this on the door of a shower at a youth hostel in Guangzhou.

Grave humour

While of a slightly morbid nature, this sign at a hospital near Wigan in England had Johan Kotze (Rondebosch) and his friends in stitches—and, no, they didn't pop in for a visit.

It seemed to Peter du Plessis (White River) that this could be more of a parting shot than an advert for the futures market. His photo was taken in Nelspruit, on the road to Barberton.

Eddie Hawkey (Potchefstroom) found it fairly typical of his town council to erect a sign like this at the entrance to the cemetery. (Translation: Graveyard only—Dead end.)

What a way to get away: HP de Bruin of Groblersdal found the contradiction in the sign and the sticker on this vehicle quite amusing. We have to agree!

While passing through Riversdale, Kobus Venter (Pretoria) came across this sign and just couldn't help wondering whether the local pistol club had an exceptionally high turnover of members.

Although the Koekemoer family (Gardenview) sent us this photo without any covering letter, we assume the place was only half the size of the Maritzburg cemetery but twice as dead.

Harry Braun (Claremont) photographed this sign outside Lamberts Bay, on the road to Clanwilliam, with the feeling that this ghoulish reminder could be too late for some unfortunate people!

Grave humour

Jan Willem and Marina Groenevelt (Ferney-Voltaire, France) feel Ramalema Driving School in Lesotho needs a new marketing manager.

Some graves in the Ciskei are fenced off to keep grazing cattle away, but that doesn't explain why the bodies are in pieces—from Peter Zeh (Kirchheim, Germany).

"Does this photo—taken en route to Pretoria on the N4—indicate what happens to all of the tech's unsuccessful students?" asks Johan de Waal (Rustenburg).

And you thought Robber's Grave was the only famous grave in Pilgrim's Rest? John Scroochy found this one at a filling station on the town's main drag.

After seeing this, Terry Terblanche (Lynnwood) realised the town fathers of Naseby in New Zealand restrict the movements of the local ghosts!

Joyce Bissett (Tzaneen) didn't hang around long enough between 11 pm and 6 am to see what happens at this spooky graveyard in Whitby, Yorkshire.

After seeing this sign, Mrs J Engelberts (Villiersdorp) couldn't help wondering whether you can camp on your way to heaven.

Have you ever felt you could die for a Coke? If so, Mrs D Grimsehl (Waterkloof) has found just the place for you . . . in Venda.

Humour from the car

Sometimes you have to look for a sign, but in Gent in Belgium you have a whole forest of them: Gent-leman Creve Willy photographed them for us.

Pam Snipe (Kirstenhof) knew precisely where she was while hiking in Surrey, England, recently.

Which way is further, the English way or the Afrikaans? This sign puzzled an observant Nico and Hermi Hoting (Mossel Bay).

All roads lead to Seagulls! Fom Bev Steele (Sloane Park).

From Rogan Bayley (Northriding).

From Mike Ratcliffe (Stellenbosch).

From Bo Nillsson (Nelspruit).

From Anne Schamotta (Raedene).

From Dr Walter Marx (Mülheim, Germany).

Humour from the car

The traditional huts in Attie Coetzee's (Plettenberg Bay) photo give it away. This isn't the way to an English mansion where carols are sung, but to Hole in the Wall in the old Transkei.

Sue and Mike Soroczynski (Swakopmund), who passed this sign many times without noticing the error, hope not all Namibian signmakers are dyslexic.

Like Bertus Meiring, we can only speculate whether Cape Sports also sails, cycles and paddles backwards.

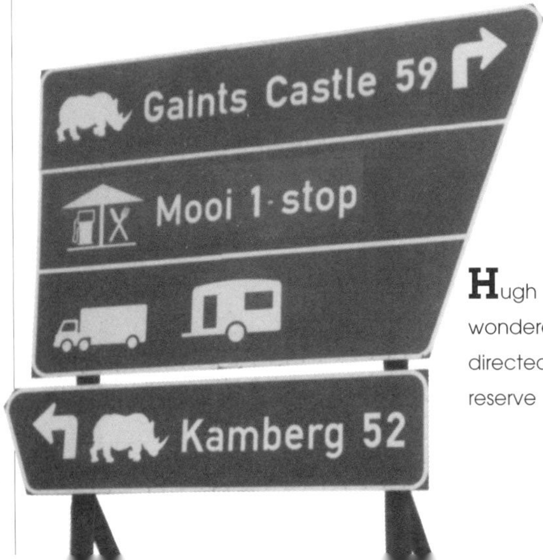

Hugh Bulcock (Howick) wondered whether this sign directed tourists to a new game reserve in the Drakensberg.

You'll find this sign, captured by Elsie Baird (East London), just outside Harrismith—but try as we may, we still can't find Bleomfontein.

Jeremy Clarke (Parkhurst) photographed this sign in a car park in County Galway, Ireland (where else!).

No further comment needed: this sign was photographed by Mike and Val Jaffe (Franschhoek) near Hartswater in the former Bophuthatswana.

It looks as though this Namibian anti-litter sign is about to become litter itself, but Dave Dominy (Westville) believes biodegradable signs have their place in our over-populated, over-littered world.

Humour from the car

Margaret Kirsten (Durban) came across this sign while hiking near Semonkong in Lesotho, so she carried on a 'couple of hills couple of bends. . . .'

Heeding this warning on the road to Semonkong, Liz and Larry Mills carefully negotiated the 'trouble some bridges' and kept their sump intact.

H Kahle (La Montagne) couldn't resist heeding this friendly advice at roadworks near Keetmanshoop, Namibia.

Annie Benade (Pretoria) discovered the pitfall when a career bureaucrat is asked to compose road signs.

Apparently the pot-holes in Zimbabwe are so bad they burst! We've received many similar photos to this one taken by Charlie Greenwood (Harare).

At this hospital in Lobatse, Botswana, you must be desperate to visit the sick . . . and also take your own bulldozer, advises Gawie Swart (Roodepoort).

Perhaps you don't notice the Free State pot-holes if you fly over them at 180 km/h? Anneen Erasmus (Strand) found a strip of black plastic tape had altered the information.

On entering Rusape in Eastern Zimbabwe, Caryn Bull (Harare) was bewildered by these confusing signs and drove at 60 km/h—just in case. . . .

A number of readers, including Mike Terry (Hermannsburg), have sent us a photo of this disquieting sign outside Louis Trichardt.

A sign of the times photographed by Alan Blem—among other sign hunters—on the outskirts of Ventersdorp.

Humour from the car

No road? No kidding! Christine Schwarz photographed this for us in Matusadona National Park, Zimbabwe.

BN Mackenzie (Pinelands) didn't know whether to go forwards or backwards when coming across this sign near the entrance of the West Coast National Park near Saldanha Bay.

This old sign just west of Schweizer-Renecke sent a very clear warning to Christiaan Terblanche (Reivilo).

In Cape Town they still give you time to kiss your partner good bye before you drive off to work. From Belinda Harker (Edgemead).

We're not sure what amused us the most, the sign photographed near Mariental, Namibia, by Lisa Berl (Windhoek), or her cheeky daughter, Natascha.

Decisions, decisions . . . ! John Willcocks (Nelspruit) stopped to take this on the Zambian side of Victoria Falls.

Karen Holm (Fontainebleau) found this 'no-entry' sign, with its interesting use of English and Afrikaans, at the Winkelspruit offramp, just south of Durban.

Humour from the car

Bronwen Ferraz (Gardens) asks if anyone could shed some light on what motorists passing this sign in Zimbabwe's Eastern Highlands should be aware of—Pacmen?

This hilarious sign photographed by Craig Nancarrow (East London) doesn't quite say what it means. See if you get the drift, albeit in a roundabout way.

André van Rensburg (Sedgefield) discovered Picasso had visted his town and changed the speed-bump warning to an 'island ahead'

No Kidding! As Penny Maddison (Rivonia) points out, this sign, which you will find just outside Walvis Bay on your way into the Namib, rather states the obvious.

Evan Douglas (Rondebosch) was looking out for elephants in Lake Mutirikwi Park in Zimbabwe, when she was surprised to come across this sign.

Petro Combrinck (Vereeniging) came across this altered sign outside Victoria Falls and couldn't decide which version was more bizarre.

An explicit warning sign photographed in Wynberg, Western Cape, by Rollo Dickson (Somerset West).

Ludwig Diener (Bethlehem) drove cautiously through this speedy gate at the entrance to the Valley of Desolation.

Max Hoppi knew he had entered a surfer's paradise at Cape St Francis when he saw this speed-hump sign had been altered by an enthusiastic waxie.

Humour from the car

"Do the children driving vehicles in Royal Natal National Park have to watch out for adults or animals?" asks GW Theunissen (Westville).

'Caution, children (and chickens) crossing': this sign, shot by JH Cragg (Linkhills), was erected by concerned but innovative parents in Molweni, KwaZulu-Natal.

Another contradictory sign: D de Jager (Chinhoyi, Zimbabwe) photographed this between Chinhoyi and Harare—the warning is presumably for the pedestrians.

This sign near Kariba, Zimbabwe, has made many *Getaway* readers grab their cameras. Craig Linden (Kloof) was one of them.

Taken near Victoria Falls, Zimbabwe, by TW Backman (Kloof).

Taken at Thompson Vlei, near Mutare, Zimbabwe, by Debbie Gorman (Mutare).

Taken in Swaziland by Jimmy Stone (address unknown).

Taken on the Bulawayo–Victoria Falls road, by Helga Eickmann (Köln, Germany).

Humour from the car

Taken in Sedgefield, near Knysna, by Dot Aves (Kleinmond).

Taken at Paddagang Restaurant, Tulbagh, by Sylvia McCallum (Benmore).

Taken in Itala Game Reserve, KwaZulu-Natal, by Mrs C Mockford (Hillcrest).

Taken in Sussex, England, and sent in by Iain and Emma Guthrie (Umhlali).

Taken in Noordhoek, near Cape Town, by Kevin Iles (Monte Vista).

Clever cows taken near Golden Gate by Vanessa Jones (Pretoria).

Taken in the Cape Winelands, by Helga Eickmann (Köln, Germany).

Taken in Cornwall, England, by Alan Wood (Stellenbosch).

Taken near De Doorns, Western Cape, by DT Swart (Saxonwold).

Animals and the environment

A gentle message to keep the crowds away: placed by the Smitswinkel Bay Residents Association and Wildlife Society, photographed by Kevin Iles (Monte Vista).

This humorous appeal, was photographed by John Hosking (Sunninghill) at Chimfunshi Wildlife Orphanage in Zambia.

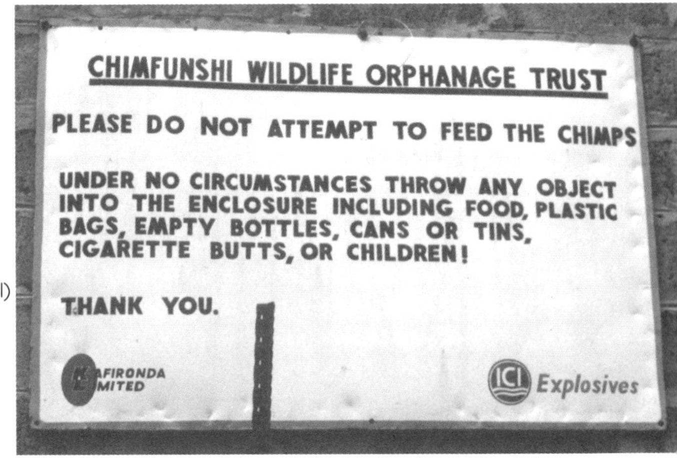

Reader S MacPherson (Umhlanga) thought this sign, in Umdloti, would be a good one for the minister of justice to take note of.

Another humorous appeal was photographed this time by John Willcocks (Nelspruit) at the camp site at Great Zimbabwe.

Derrick de Necker (Uvongo) would like to know whether this seagull is policing this sign at Hermanus, or just can't understand why no one is feeding him.

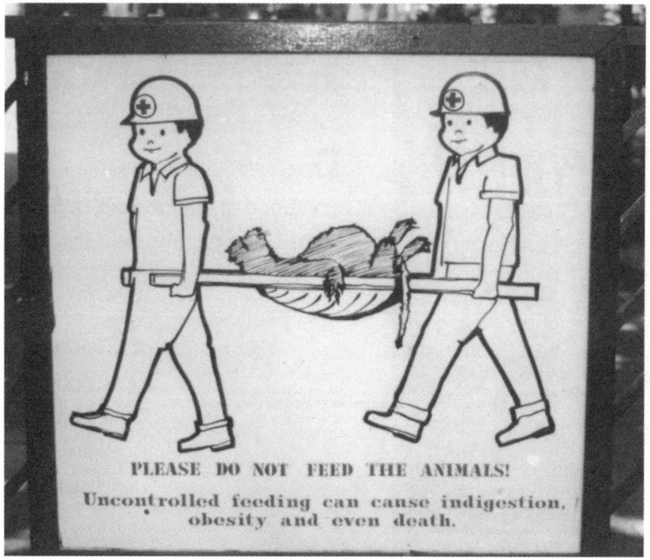

This sign was seen by Mrs Moolman (Wierda Park), but she didn't tell us where.

Bet you didn't know baboons were a great delicacy in the Cape Peninsula? Ray Kruger (Welkom) couldn't resist a taste.

Animals and the environment

In Holland there are places where dogs can't *poep* (below, from Eddie Tiemensma in Secunda) and where they can (left, from Oda van der Kemp in Pretoria).

Dogs in Scotland cannot claim ignorance of the law as a defence—as recorded (again!) by Eddie Tiemensma (Secunda).

A Swiss dog toilet photographed by Mr EK Kesseli (Pretoria). How long 'till they start using cell phones?

Paulie Marais shows off one of the most popular signs in the *Getaway* collection. Photographed in the Wilderness Lakes Area by André Gouws (Johannesburg).

Wilna Calitz (Wonderboompoort) was pleasantly surprised at the pet facilities at Exel Stop garage on the N4 Witbank Freeway near Bronkhorstspruit.

Val White (Bryanston) came across this sign en route to Cape Town and was amazed to discover pet owners are teaching their dogs to read.

Animals and the environment

This photo was taken at the hotel at De Kelders near Hermanus by Ms A Mansfield (Klerksdorp).

"They really are serious about not allowing dogs on the beach at Herold's Bay," advises Anka Grobler (George).

"Only in England would you find a sign like this," says Ceri Jones (Devon, England) who took this shot in the southwest.

Denise Horner (Berea) found this thoughtful refreshment point while out walking recently.

"You may alight here from your vehicle at your own risk. . . ." Photographer Karin Flobbe (Benoni) never took the risk.

Back in the 60s, Mr E Kesseli (Milner Park) came across this sign in Kenya.

Cheryl Daffen (New South Wales) couldn't grab her camera quick enough after turning into the drive at Tshukudu Game Lodge in Hoedspruit.

"Who says lions don't walk around Cape Town anymore?" Greg Olsen (Marina da Gama), captured this in the Tokai Forest.

Animals and the environment

Val Kendall (Bulawayo, Zimbabwe) thought other readers might like to share her amusement at this sign near her home.

Diane Dolpire (Hilton) had heard of watchdogs, but never watchhorses, before seeing this near Howick in KwaZulu-Natal.

Deon Ferreira (Centurion) was amazed by the social antics of horses on the Stellenbosch Wine Route.

"Apparently the horses in Botswana have an above-average IQ," comments an amused Cecilé Reed (Bloemfontein).

Michael and Eleanor Pretorius (Ceres) asked the old man what this sign on the side of Lake Baringo in Kenya implied, but no communication was possible.

On safari in Sweetwaters Game Reserve near Mount Kenya, a group of travellers took this for *Getaway*. Carryn Wiltshire's (Sunningdale) was the first to arrive.

'Deer oh deer': A van Rensburg (Hillcrest) caught this message on the road between Harrismith and Johannesburg.

An obedient little steenbok photographed by Lucas Smith (Benoni) between Satara and Olifants in the Kruger Park.

Animals and the environment

Mark Shnaps and Peggy Rabb came across this warning in the Perinet Reserve, Madagascar.

'Please bring me another tourist, the last one was delicious . . .' states this sign photographed by Magdalene Louw (Paarl) at Sun City.

"Could it be the big one?" asks HM van Rooyen (Waterkloof).

A mutch-photographed sign at the crocodile centre at St Lucia taken by Eugene Nel (Ballito).

A popular sign at Victoria Falls photographed by Graham Waugh (Fourways).

A reader who wished to remain anonymous came across this sign for educated seagulls in Saldanha, on the Western Cape coast.

And you have to walk 10 kilometres to get there, discovered Kelvin Trautman (Hilton).

An unusual sign captured near Bristol, England, by Mrs RA Everitt (Mulbarton).

Johann du Plessis (Pretoria) stopped at this warning sign north of Perth in Scotland and, sure enough, the birds were there.

Animals and the environment

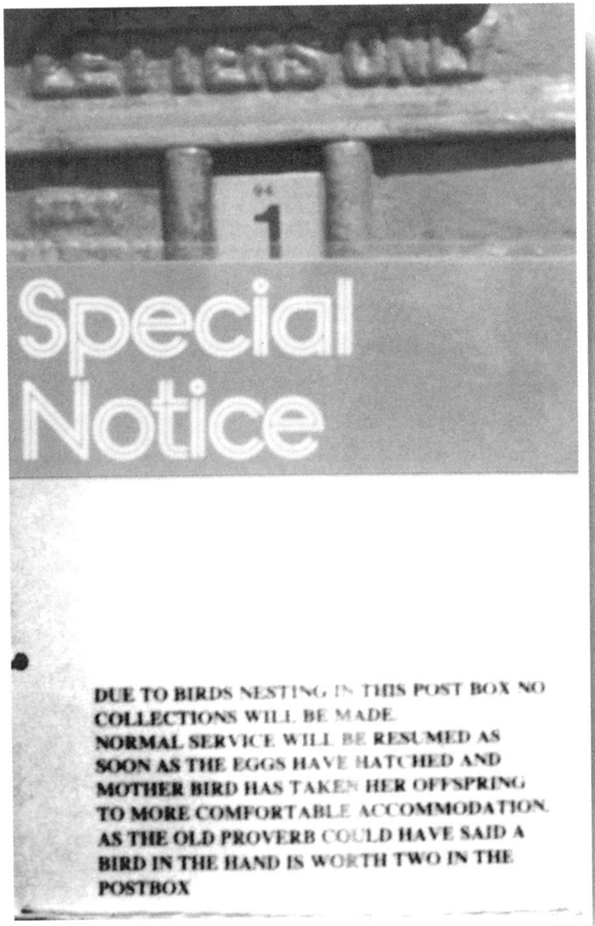

The postal authorities in the UK sure have a high regard for their local wildlife, points out CR Botha (Durban).

As sharp-eyed Peter Lloyd (Plettenberg Bay) discovered, the residents of Noordhoek, near Cape Town, expect every chicken to do its duty.

Although the zebras near Oudtshoorn disguise themselves fantastically well, they didn't fool Graham Foxton (Sunninghill).

This strange sign, taken by the Stephenson family (Glenashley) at St Lucia, is one of the most-photographed we receive.

Like Johannes de Wet (Steel), we're not quite sure what happens to the trees and plants at Mlilwane Wildlife Sanctuary near Mbabane.

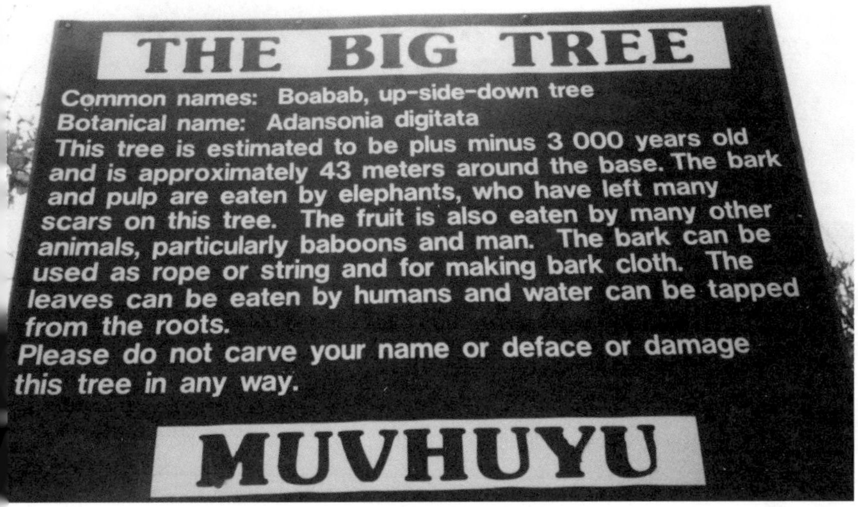

Johann and Wilemien de Wet (Cullinan) snapped this 'up-side-down tree' information board in Venda, complete with the 'up-side-down sign' that goes with it.

Animals and the environment

If you miss this sign, taken by Veronica Coetzer (Pretoria) near Gwanda in Zimbabwe, how do you explain the resulting damage to your insurance company?

What is worse than trees in the middle of the road? Trees that move themselves there, according to Lara Nel and Pieter Fourie (Hatfield).

Thanks for the timely warning! We're not sure whether Mrs R Muller (Pretoria) was caught out or not.

This sign, recorded near her home by Karen Puchert (Stutterheim), stands at the foot of the Amatola Mountains.

Jenny Bunge (Hurlyvale) asks if this sign between Beit Bridge and Masvingo is Zimbabwe's contribution to genetic engineering.

When the waters of the Vaal Dam rose, they left a funny sign to amuse André and Wendy Lochner of Cape Town.

It's the waters of Buffelspoort Dam near Rustenburg that have risen this time, amusing Des and Michelle Erasmus (Kroondal).

Telling it like it is near Ondangwa in Ovamboland, Namibia. This scene was captured by several readers, including D Phillips (Namibia).

Now you know the secret of the great golfers of northern KwaZulu-Natal—they lick their balls. From golfer Stefan Cilliers (Ingogo).

"Say, Honey, is this Africa?
(Little bits of Africa in other continents.)

Heather Shearer (Aurora) wondered whether Eugene Terreblanche knew about this sign she saw on a church in Christchurch, New Zealand.

Having become skilled at ignoring persuasive carpet shop owners in Turkey, Susan Williams (Luipaardsvlei) found herself at the mercy of the owner of this one in Selçuk—drinking apple tea and hanging on to her wallet.

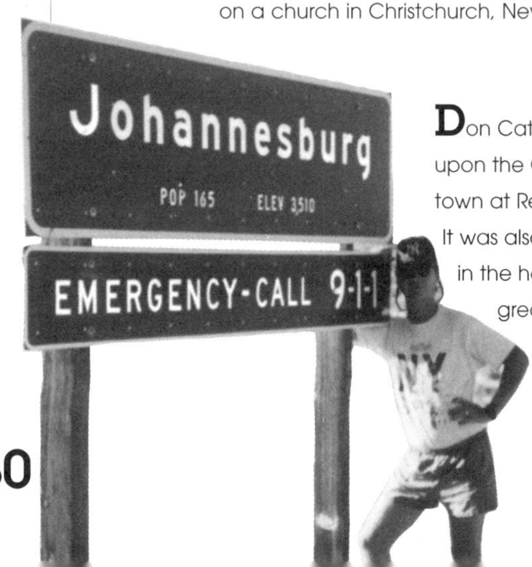

Don Cater (Silverton) stumbled upon the Gauteng capital's twin town at Red Rock Canyon, California. It was also a gold-rush town, named in the hope that it, too, would yeild great riches. Unfortunately the place and population never really boomed.

While working in Turkey for a few years, MB Hunter (Bryanston) chanced upon this village name sign in the southwestern region. Since the name seemed quite appropriate, he decided not to stop over.

"Honey, are you *sure* this is Africa?
(Little bits of other continents in Africa.)

Although perhaps not what the England poet Rupert Brooke had in mind, Dudley Walker (Edenvale) found this intriguing short cut on the road between Olifantshoek and Kuruman in the Northern Cape.

Wim Belgraver (Sasolburg) encountered this sign in Kestell. Unfortunately his hiking party was so snowed in they couldn't discover where the sign promised.

"Who says the Northern Province hasn't got it all?" asks Sue Rautenbach (Waterpoort), who took this photo on the R519 en route to Pietersburg.

North America

Walter Richards (Denver, Colorado) immediately thought of fellow *Getaway* readers when he passed this warning on Interstate 60, Arizona.

Adin and Sharon Greaves (Swellendam) were out in the sticks in Nevada when they found this road.

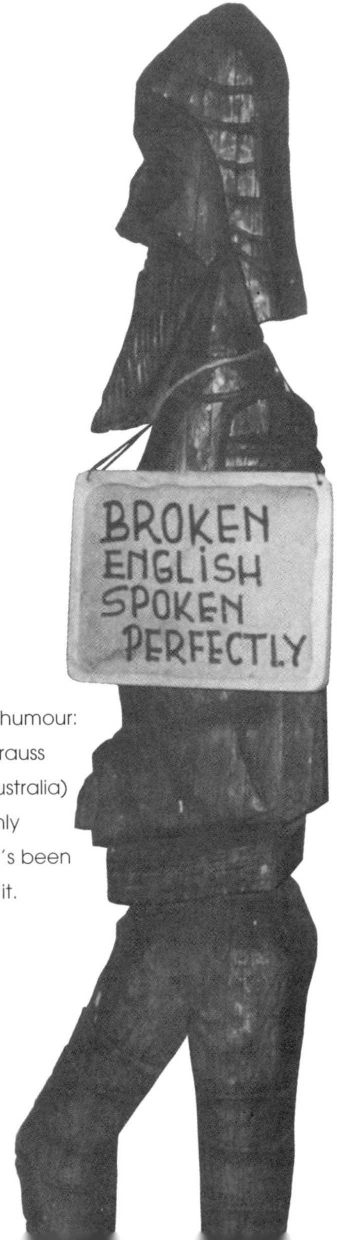

Mexican humour: Prudence Krauss (Victoria, Australia) is not our only reader who's been there, seen it.

Rob and Julia Buchanan (Kirstenhof) explain there's a town called Boring in Oregon in the States. The state, however, was anything but.

When looking for his cousin in California, J Engelbrecht immediately knew he'd found him when he saw this number plate.

Keith Fahrenfort (Houston, Texas) found this sign in his local neighbourhood.

Nallie Louw (Pretoria) tells us the snow at Lake Tahoe, California, was two metres deep when she took this photo.

During a recent trip to the USA, Guy Bompass chanced upon this ghoulish cafeteria.

Photographer Colin Mead found this classic (one of our all-time favourites) in Jackson Hole in Wyoming state.

Britain

Charles and Pat Buckley (West Sussex, England) took 'moor care' when exploring the Dartmoor wilderness area.

Prof Fraser Ross (Edgemead) enjoyed the British humour in this sign photographed in Hersham, Surrey.

Another example of British humour, uncovered by André and Rina van der Merwe (Somerset, England) in the Exmoor district of Southwest England.

This photograph was taken at St Andrews, the home of golf, in Scotland, by Peter Hocknell (Kensington).

Pauline Harding (Wellington) found this notice near Dunluce Castle, Northern Ireland, typically Irish.

Dr Jean du Toit (Wartburg) came across this 'warning' while working as a vet among the dangerous animals of North Wales.

Rudi de Groot (Sandton) took heed and slowed down at this sign in Scotland.

Still in Scotland, Glynne and Charlene Brand (Onrus River) found this on Edinburgh's Royal Mile.

"This call is for ewe," another photo from Rudi de Groot's (Sandton) Scottish collection.

Adéle van der Merwe couldn't see any ponies while travelling through Cumbria, just hundreds of sheep. . . .

Australia and New Zealand

Dr and Mrs DH Davy observed this sign while visiting their daughter in McKay in Queensland.

David Turner (Kloof) took this photo while holidaying in Northern Queensland, Australia.

Tony Oosthuysen (Bethlehem) enjoyed this sign at the caravan park at Roturoa in New Zealand.

Ann Steenkamp (Clanwilliam) came across this frank offer while driving through the outskirts of Melbourne.

"Railway personnel had recently moved out of the town of Cook, on the Nullarbor Plain of Australia," explains Graham Atkinson (Hilton). "But the appeal for clients didn't work and the hospital soon closed down."

On a recent visit to New Zealand, CR Willows (Cowies Hill) chanced upon these thought-provoking signs.

"This was a very apt sign," remarked Mrs W Huggins (Hillary) who took the photo on South Island, New Zealand.

Nina Bailey (Somerset West) took heed of this blunt warning behind a petrol station on South Island, New Zealand . . .

. . . While Tim Davis (Auckland, New Zealand) found landowners are also quite blunt on North Island.

"The behaviour of the monkeys in the Monkey Forest on the island Bali, Indonesia, was not as bad as that of the humans," advises Pieter Siebert (Newlands).

Jill Goldkorn (Craighall) was careful to observe the rules printed on this sign at the Great Wall of China near Beijing.

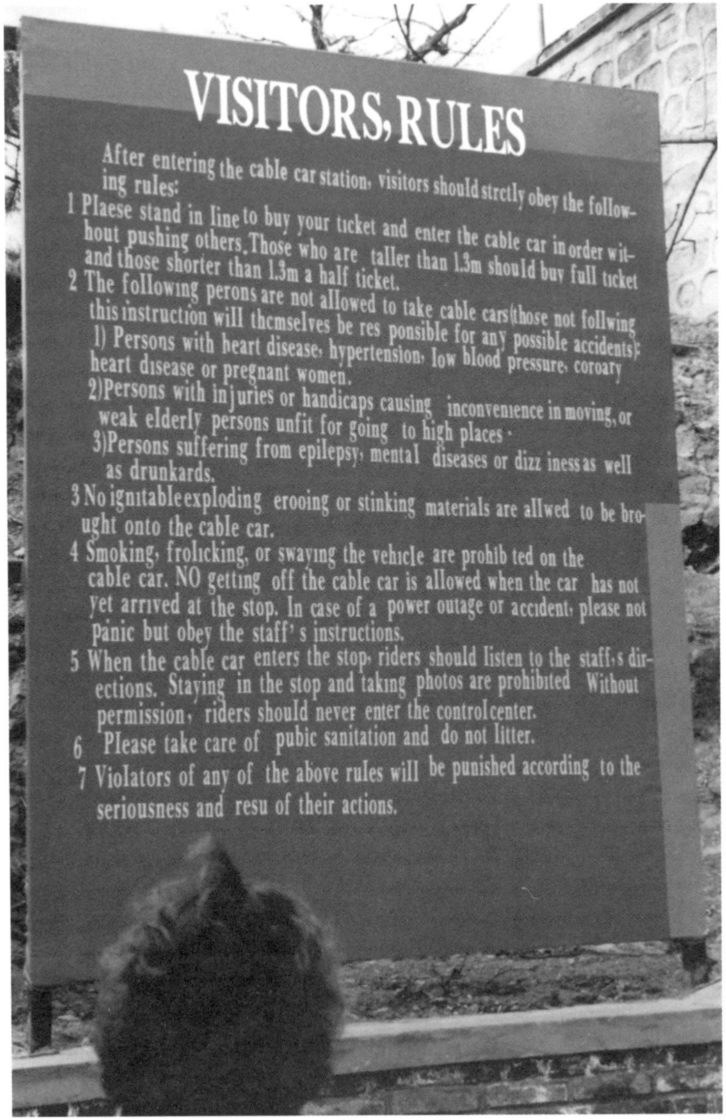

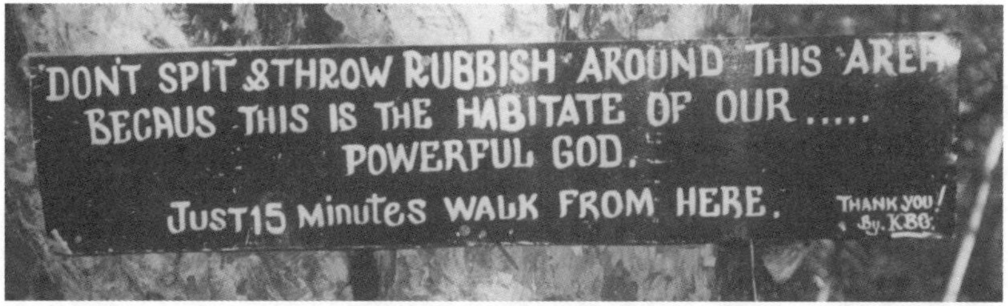

Taken by Ottilie Neser (Pretoria) in the Annapurna region of the Himalayas.

Taken by Heather Denton (Fourways) near Kuala Lumpur.

Taken by Kenneth Carden (Constantia) in Chiang Rai in Thailand.

Taken by `expert' HO Reuter of Windhoek, in Beijing, China.

Taken by Johan Slabbert (Centurion) on the island of Koh Samui, Thailand.

Taken by NH Bazeley (Rondebosch East) on the island of Phuket, Thailand.

Taken by Leigh Voigt (Schagen) in Nepal.

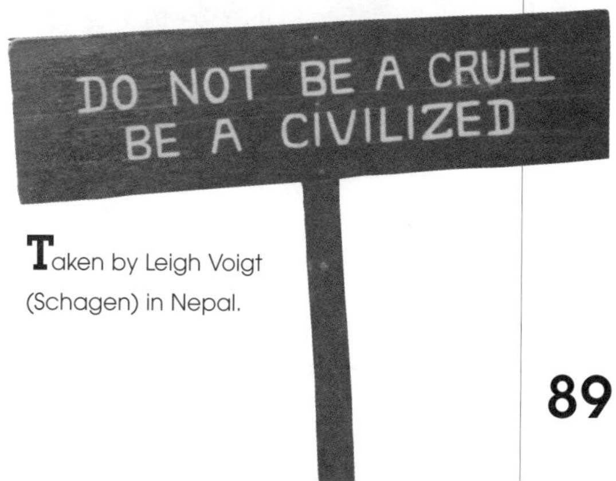

Taken by Leigh Voigt (Schagen) in Nepal.

Far East

"Fat what!" Taken in Jerantut, Malaysia by an anonymous reader.

A sign for South African *breekers*? Peter van Heerden (Mayville) found it on the edge of a wadi (river) while on a holiday in Oman.

This sign on Lamma Island just south of Hong Kong was appropriate for Robyn Cullis (seen with brother James in the photo) who was awaiting her matric results. From Dr Sydney Cullis (Claremont).

"What a bargain!" Taken in Taiwan by Samuel Kemp (Secunda).

"Could have his uses!" Taken in Hong Kong by Geoff Rutter (Magalies View).

One last laugh

"The municipality calls this locked?" Photographed by Gina Hagen (Hibberdene) on a farm between Strand and Gordon's Bay

"At least the sign prevented burning on the left-hand side of the road between Bethlehem and Ladysmith," remarked Werner Bermeister (Montagu).

Neville Odell (Fourways) found this entertaining sign at the start of a trail through the Crystal Springs Mountain Lodge resort in Mpumalanga.

"How far should one go when obeying this sign in New Orleans?" asks Julie Toffoli (Rivonia).

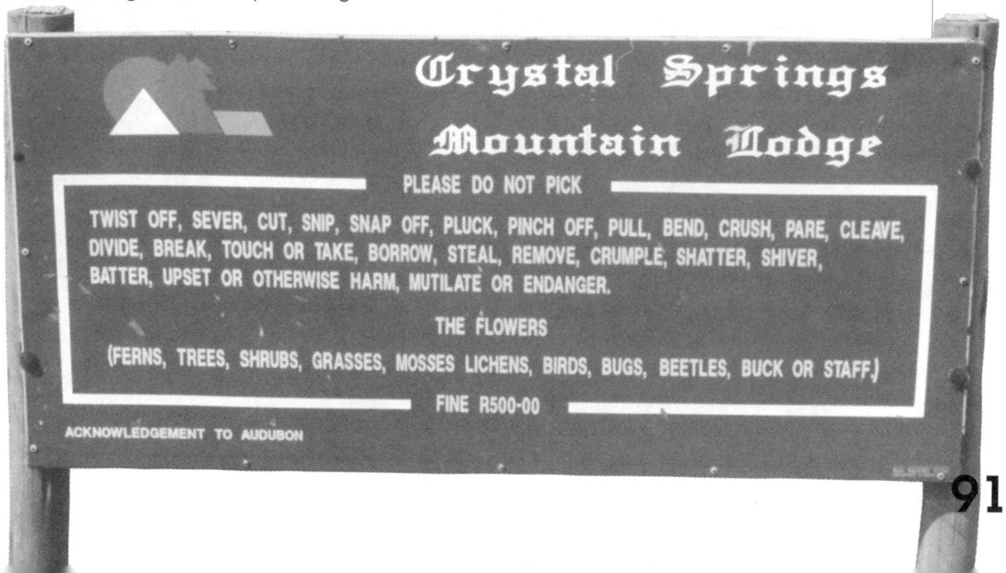

One last laugh

"Ag, shame!*"* Anton Meyer (Bethal) photographed this polite request—not to park on the farmer's maize—between Ogies and Balmoral in Mpumalanga.

Mike Jordaan (Berndorf, Austria) dreads the thought of what could happen to any hiker who doesn't heed this sign at Giants Castle in the KwaZulu-Natal Drakensberg.

"You turn your back for a moment and look what happens!" Sent in by Mr K Zunckel (Nelspruit).

And the National Party wondered why its support plummeted in Pretoria, reader PS van der Westhuizen's home town?

Is it just Robert Niemann, or do other readers find something amusing about this poster he photographed in Harare?

Poor Marthinus again: Judy Havemann (Port Elizabeth) found this combination along Port Elizabeth's beachfront.

One last laugh

"If you're Afrikaans you can't, if you're English you can?" Photographed at Aventura Warmbad by F Ruddeck (Carolina).

Brendan Stewart (Pinetown) found this sign at the Cuddle Puddle Health Spa, next to Royal Swazi Sun.

"If you had a name like this would you advertise it?" Taken by Donald and Wendy MacKenzie (St Francis Bay) on Praslin, in the Seychelles.

Nell-Marie Joubert (Pretoria) tells us this sign is larger than the bakery it advertises in Mozambique, while the bread is "lovely".

Funny Signs order form ● *Getaway* subscription form

Use a photocopy of the coupon below to order additional copies of *Funny Signs*.
You can also subscribe to *Getaway* magazine and get 12 local issues of the best holiday, adventure-travel and ecotourism magazine in Africa for just R124 (including VAT and postage).

Getaway
Places to go, things to do.

Complete this and post it to: *Getaway*, PO Box 596, Howard Place 7450, Cape Town.

Yes! **Please send me *Funny Signs* @ R29,95 each.**

I'd like ☐ 1 copy ☐ 2 copies
☐ 3 copies ☐ other (please specify)..........................

Yes! **I'll subscribe to *Getaway*.**
Please send me 12 issues for only R124*.

This is a:
☐ new subscription
☐ subscription renewal
☐ R124* for a local subscription
☐ R269 for a foreign surface subscription
☐ R398 for a foreign airmail subscription

My details are: (please print)
Title ....Name ....
Postal Address ....
....Code. ....
Work tel (.............).......................Home tel (.............) ....
e-mail ....

Send a gift subscription of *Getaway* to:
Title ....Name..
Postal Address ....
....Code ....

Payment details: ☐ cheque
☐ credit card

Card no ☐☐☐☐ ☐☐☐☐ ☐☐☐☐ ☐☐☐☐

Expiry Date ☐☐☐☐
m m y y

Signature ....

ID no ☐☐☐☐☐☐ ☐☐☐☐ ☐☐☐

Offer valid while stocks last

gfs/inbook

Subscriber Helpline (0860) 100 205, fax (021) 531-7303 or e-mail subsmail@rsp.co.za

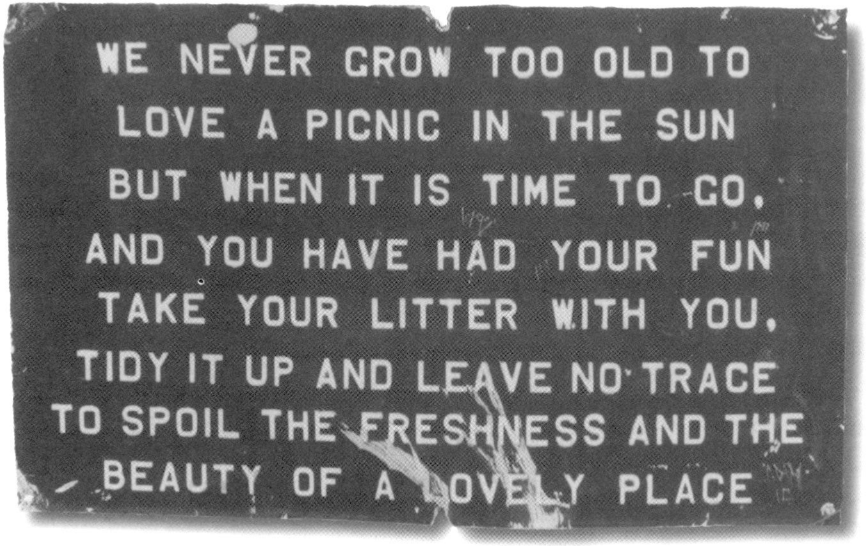

Photographed at Union's End (the remotest spot in South Africa) by AA Swanepoel (Pierre van Ryneveld).